Baltimore's
COUNTRY COUSINS

SUSAN
McKELVEY

Album Quilt Patterns

 American Quilter's Society
P. O. Box 3290 • Paducah, KY 42002-3290
www.AmericanQuilter.com

Located in Paducah, Kentucky, the American Quilter's Society (AQS) is dedicated to promoting the accomplishments of today's quilters. Through its publications and events, AQS strives to honor today's quiltmakers and their work and to inspire future creativity and innovation in quiltmaking.

EDITOR: BARBARA SMITH
GRAPHIC DESIGN: ELAINE WILSON
COVER DESIGN: MICHAEL BUCKINGHAM
ILLUSTRATIONS: AMY CHASE
PHOTOGRAPHY: CHARLES R. LYNCH

Library of Congress Cataloging-in-Publication Data

McKelvey, Susan Richardson.

Baltimore's country cousins : album quilt patterns / by Susan McKelvey.

p. cm.

Summary: "Instructions for making 12 appliqué blocks in Baltimore Album style. Includes tips on fabric selection, block variations and borders. Section on writing and stamping on quilts including ink embellishments"--Provided by publisher.

Includes bibliographical references.

ISBN 1-57432-905-7

1. Appliqué.   I. Title.

TT779.M387 2006

746.44'5--dc22

2005037425

Additional copies of this book may be ordered from the American Quilter's Society, PO Box 3290, Paducah, KY 42002-3290; 800-626-5420 (orders only please); or online at www.AQSquilt.com. For all other inquiries, call 270-898-7903.

Proudly printed and bound in the United States of America

Dedication

Dedicated to Luke Michael Adelman, our first precious grandchild.
Welcome to the comforting world of quilts and books.

SPRING GLORY, 36" x 36", made by the author

Baltimore's Country Cousins, 66" x 82", made by the author

Contents

Introduction

Appliqué album quilts became popular along the eastern seaboard in the early nineteenth century. In these multi-block quilts, each block contained a different pictorial design, taken from decorative objects of the period: bouquets of flowers, fruit set in vases, and baskets and urns surrounded by bows and swags. In some of the quilts, the blocks are divided by sashing, usually in a red fabric or a printed stripe. The borders are often made from large prints or embellished with swags and decorative dogtooth or scalloped edges.

The appliqué album quilts vary in sophistication, but in the brief period from the mid 1830s to the late 1850s, a particularly elegant quilt style took over the city of Baltimore and its surrounding counties. The resulting quilts have become known as "Baltimore Album Quilts."

Many of these elegant pieces were made by groups of women as presentation quilts, and the blocks were sometimes created by professional designers. As the album quilt style became popular and spread to outlying areas of Maryland, it was altered and sometimes simplified. We often see quilts that are Baltimore in style but less elegant, containing the same elements but in simpler, more primitive forms. These tend to come from the rural counties of eastern and central Maryland and southern Pennsylvania, and they harken back to the earlier album quilts. It is these simple, whimsical country quilts that appeal to me and that lured me to design BALTIMORE'S COUNTRY COUSINS. I hope you will enjoy working with these designs as much as I have.

FABRIC *Selection*

An album quilt by definition contains many different blocks. When choosing fabrics for an album quilt, you need to consider how to tie these diverse blocks together. The Country Cousins patterns are already united in style and scale, and you can add to the unity of your quilt through the use of color.

For my version of BALTIMORE'S COUNTRY COUSINS, I chose bright, strong colors and traditional prints reminiscent of those popular in the 1850s' folksy album quilts of Maryland and Pennsylvania, but the blocks will be lovely in any color scheme. The color schemes range from dramatic, bright colorings to soft, muted combinations, and they all look wonderful. The varied treatments of these country blocks show just how timeless the designs are. Go with your heart as you choose your colors.

TRY A THEME FABRIC

It helps to find a fabric you love that contains many colors (fig. 1). Often, this fabric is a large-scale print. Fabric designers are experts at creating pleasing color combinations, so if you like the colors in the theme fabric, you will like a quilt made from these colors.

In addition to pulling colors from the theme fabric, try using small pieces of this fabric in various appliqué elements. This is an easy way to tie the elements in your quilt together. If you don't want to appliqué the border, look for a theme fabric instead. A theme fabric will make a wonderful border because it ties all the colors together, completing the fabric picture and providing a frame full of contrast and unity.

Fig. 1. Example of a theme fabric

Fig. 2. Contrast: (a) subtle, (b) vibrant

Fig. 3. BALTIMORE ON THE LESS TRAVELED BACK ROADS, 50" x 50", by Jan Carlson

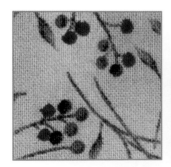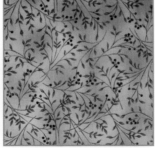

Fig. 4. Look at this sweet print. It contains two values of green with tiny bright blue and red berries. Close up it is pretty and detailed, but from a distance it reads as a green print because the berries are so tiny.

USE CONTRAST AND VARIETY

Obviously, you should choose fabrics, colors, and color combinations that please you. Strive for unity, contrast, and variety to unify your quilt. Using the patterns as your style base, decide how you want your version of BALTIMORE'S COUNTRY COUSINS to look and what color scheme and kinds of fabric will create this vision.

For example, do you want a dramatic quilt, full of bright colors, or a soft, faded-looking quilt, reminiscent of an antique? No matter what style you choose, include contrast. Contrast may be low (subtle) or high (vibrant), as we see in the two variations of the Basket of Bluebells block. In my version, I used cool blues and greens with a soft gold-beige basket, creating a quiet, delicate color scheme. What a contrast we see in Candy's version. She created a strong warm-cool contrast with blue and green in the background, leaves, and basket set against bright yellow and orange flowers (fig. 2).

REPEAT COLORS

When you use a color in several places, especially a strong color, it creates visual movement, drawing the viewer's eyes across the quilt (fig. 3). Choosing a color scheme for an album quilt challenges you to repeat colors in many different blocks, but keep in mind that, if you use a lot of a color in one block, echo it in smaller amounts in other blocks. A dab of color will have an eye-catching effect.

Notice that I am talking about color, not fabric. It doesn't matter whether the tiny green leaves in a red print fabric are the same green as in another fabric because, from five feet away, the fabric "reads" as red. The leaves will be lovely details for close admiration, but what matters is the color seen from a distance (fig. 4).

MIX LEAF AND STEM FABRICS

To create variety and texture within a block, use several different fabrics and prints for the leaves and stems (fig. 5). To create unity within the entire quilt, scatter and repeat the different prints in several blocks.

CREATE MOVEMENT

Fabric prints can create movement. Look for shaded or mottled prints to add subtle dimension to your appliqué elements. Try striped designs to add more distinct direction (fig. 6).

SASHING AND BORDERS

I like to separate busy appliqué blocks with sashing to set off the blocks so they can be admired for themselves. Adding an inner border identical in width and color outlines the quilt center and divides it from the outer appliquéd border. IN BALTIMORE'S COUNTRY COUSINS, both the sashing and inner border are 1½" wide. Your sashing may be wider and, of course, any color. I often use a stripe on the diagonal to add movement to the quilt, freeing it from the static divided-block layout.

The outer appliquéd border repeats a variety of design elements from the blocks, thus tying the quilt center and border together. The border appliqué is designed to flow downward from the top center and along the sides to meet at the bottom center. Therefore, most of the leaves and flowers hang downward. You can change the direction and the positions of the floral elements as you like; for example, the elements can flow upward toward the top center.

For my quilt, I made a 6" wide border, repeating the white background fabric in the blocks. For the pattern instructions (starting on page 22), I improved upon this border by making it a few inches wider, so that there is more open space on either side of the vine and flowers.

Fig. 5. Leaves and stems cut from different fabrics create interest.

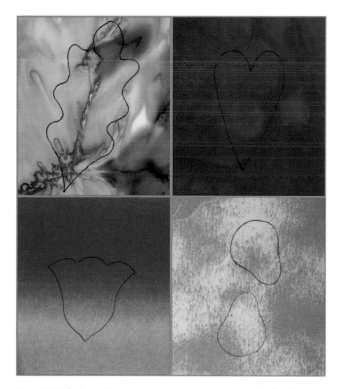

Fig. 6. Fabric prints create movement and shading.

APPLIQUÉ *Tips*

There are many excellent books for appliqué techniques. If you are new to appliqué, I recommend that you refer to one of them. Any techniques for template making, fabric marking, and sewing will work well with these blocks. Use the method you prefer.

PREPARING BACKGROUND SQUARES

I refer to all of the fabric pieces that will be appliquéd as "appliqué elements."

The following suggestions are for needle-turn appliqué:

Cut the background squares 4" larger than the desired finished size of the blocks. This way, if your appliqué is slightly askew, you can adjust and center the design when you trim the blocks to size.

Use a steam iron to mark a simple layout guide on your block background by pressing four creases in it, as shown in figure 1. These lines will provide quick and accurate positioning guides for placing your appliqué elements, and the lines can be ironed out when you have finished the appliqué.

Mark the positions of the appliqué elements on the block background. To avoid having placement marks show later, I lay the background fabric over the pattern and mark just a hint of the key shape (usually a significant curve or a base position) in several places, approximately ⅛" inside the actual edge of the element (fig. 2, page 11). These marks are easily covered by the appliqué elements when they are sewn. Maintain a consistent distance inside the sewing line as you mark different elements, so they keep their correct positions.

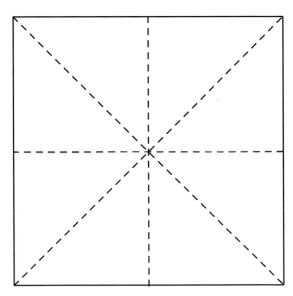

Fig. 1. Press placement guides in your block background.

MAKING TEMPLATES

Using template plastic. If an appliqué element appears multiple times, a leaf for example, make its template out of translucent template plastic. This template doesn't wear down during the marking process. Because you can see through it, you can position the template on the fabric precisely where you want, and it works well for designs that reverse, such as two facing birds, because you can flip it over.

Tracing directly on fabric. If an element is large and appears only once, you can trace it directly onto the fabric by taping the pattern over a light box or window. Then lay the fabric over the pattern and trace.

Using freezer paper. For intricate elements, you can use freezer paper ironed onto the right side of the fabric to give you an outline to mark. Leave the paper on the fabric until you have cut out the element. The contrast between the white paper and the colored fabrics makes cutting easy. Remove the paper when you sew so you are dealing with only the fabric and the turn line.

MARKING APPLIQUÉ FABRICS

Whether using plastic or freezer-paper templates or laying the appliqué fabric over a light box, draw all the sewing (turning) lines from the appliqué elements.

Use a light-colored pencil on dark fabrics and a dark-colored pencil on light fabrics. For medium-colored or busy fabrics, ones on which it is difficult to see light or dark markings, use a black or brown, fine-point, permanent pen. Permanent ink won't run, and the fine point makes a delicate line that easily disappears as you turn under the fabric.

Remember to add 3/16" (by eye) turn-under allowances to the appliqué elements as you cut them.

MAKING A STEM COLLECTION

Stems are needed for most of the blocks. You can make many stems at once, store them wrapped around a cardboard tube, and cut off the lengths as you need them (fig. 3). To start a

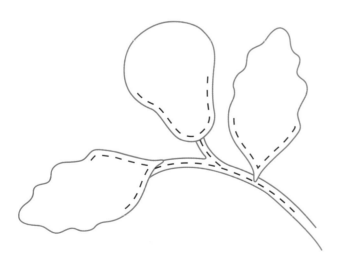

Fig. 2. The red dotted line shows where to mark the elements on the background.

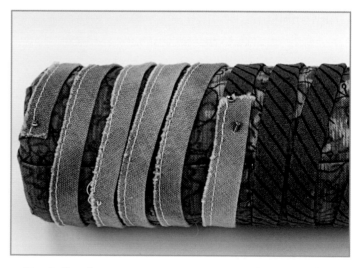

Fig. 3. Ready-to-use stems are wrapped on a cardboard tube.

collection of stems of different widths, cut long lengths of 1" wide bias strips. Press them in half lengthwise, wrong sides together.

On each folded strip, machine sew a line either ⅛" or ¼" from the folded edges and trim off the excess fabric outside the seam. Or, if you are making very slender stems, press well but don't machine sew them yet. Cut the length of stem you need as you prepare the block.

DETERMINING STITCHING SEQUENCE

With each block, there are specific directions about stitching sequence and adding details. In general, however, it helps to examine a block to see what appliqué elements control the design, then begin by sewing these elements. Consider the following sequences:

Beginning with stems. Often, the shapes of the stems define the block. Once you get the stems sewn in the correct positions, it is easy to add the other elements, adjusting them to cover the stem ends. Whether there is one defining stem, as in the Garden Medallion block, or several, as in Drooping Daisies, sew the stems first (fig. 4). Get them right and the rest of the block follows easily.

Starting with center elements. Some blocks contain large center elements, such as the house in Home Sweet Home and the heart in Beloved Heart (fig. 5). In these cases, sew the center elements first, taking into account any stems that might be tucked under them. In this way, if your house is slightly askew or larger or smaller than the pattern, you can adjust the surrounding elements accordingly.

a	b

Fig. 4. Start with stems: (a) Drooping Daisies, (b) Four Feeding Birds.

Fig. 5. Start with center elements: (a) Home Sweet Home, (b) Beloved Heart.

APPLIQUÉING THE BORDER

Cutting border strips. The appliquéd border strips are cut extra wide and long to allow for the natural pulling-in that occurs during the appliqué process. Fold and press each strip to mark the centers and the four sections of the length, plus the two corner sections, as shown in figure 6, page 13.

Marking the inside edge. Use a pencil to mark the inside edge (in the seam allowance) of each border because, once the vines have been appliquéd, the borders will look so similar that it will be easy to confuse them.

Marking the elements. To mark the vine placement on the border pieces, cut two 8" wide strips of paper, one the length of one fourth of the side edge (excluding the corner portion) and one the length of one fourth of the top edge.

Draw a line down the vertical and horizontal centers of each space. Draw a curving vine within this length of the border and experiment with the curve until you find a design you like (fig. 7). Use the vertical center line as your guide. The vine can be as curvy as you want, but keep in mind the sizes of the appliqué elements you want to tuck into it.

Be sure the vine ends in the same place at each end of the strip so it will line up when repeated in each section. When you have a design you like, go over it with a marker so it is visible through the background fabric. Then pin or tape the fabric strips over the paper and trace the pattern onto the fabric strips, making sure the vine is centered and the sections match.

Mark the key appliqué elements on the vine, such as the side hearts, top birds, and bottom center flowers. The scattered elements can be positioned as you sew.

Appliquéing the elements. Appliqué the left and right borders first, and at the same time, so they are identical but reversed. Wait to sew the corner elements onto the border until all four borders have been attached to the quilt center, so you can adjust the corner elements as needed.

When you sew the vine to the background, leave a generous tail at each end so you have plenty to work with as you adjust the vine to fit under the corner elements.

Appliqué the vine first. Sew the center border elements next. (Each side has a major center element.) Add the other flowers and leaves, which can be adjusted as needed. Be creative here, using the border pattern as a jumping-off point. Add more flowers and fewer leaves or different flowers and leaves. Use fewer bull's-eyes and more birds. Sew the corner elements last.

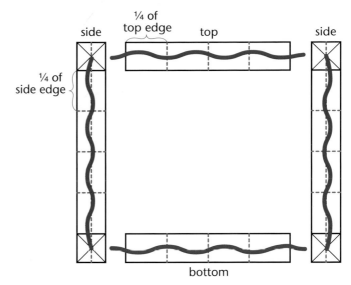

Fig. 6. Measuring and laying out the vine on the border

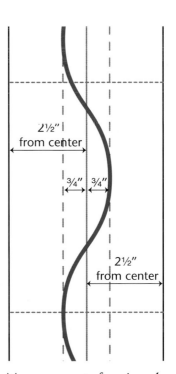

Fig. 7. Measurements for vine placement

INKING & STAMPING ON
Quilts

In the mid-nineteenth century, writing beautifully was an accomplishment American women admired, strived for, and demonstrated in their autograph books and journals and on their quilts. When we look at quilts of the period, especially Baltimore-style quilts, we see beautifully signed blocks. They were sometimes stamped, sometimes stenciled, and usually done in freehand writing. All of these methods are available to us today.

Stamped message on Birds at the Fountain
(block pattern on page 42)

WRITING ON BLOCKS

I recommend that you write on a block before you sew it. This way, if you make a mistake, you have lost only a piece of fabric.

To start, lay a piece of lined paper over the pattern and draw an outline of the space you have available for writing on your block. Draw a line down the center. Trace several copies of the outline on paper to use as practice pieces.

Practice writing and centering the lettering in the space on the copies. When you are satisfied with the writing, use a light source to trace the words on the block background or use the practice piece as a guide to write them freehand.

TRACING COMPUTER SCRIPT

For a large space, such as that in the center of Garden Medallion (page 30), I often set up the words on the computer and then trace them onto the fabric. If you aren't computer savvy, enlist the help of a friend, child, or grandchild. Follow these steps to make computer script:

1. Decide what you want to say and type it out in any font in any size. Divide the words or phrases into several lines as appropriate. These can be adjusted later. Choose "center justify" to set up a poem-like layout.

2. Measure the space on your block where you want to place your computer script. Experiment with different fonts and choose a beautiful script that you like and that is appropriate for your quilt. Make it bold because bold letters are easier to see through fabric for tracing.

3. Measure the area on your block where you want to place the computer script. Enlarge or reduce the point size of your message to fit into this area, allowing for open space around the message so it doesn't seem crowded. Print your message on lightweight paper.

4. Work over a light box and practice tracing the letters on a piece of smooth muslin before working on the background fabric. Tape the paper over the light box with removable tape. Tape the fabric over the paper, centering the message visible through the fabric. Trace *only* the outlines of all the letters.

5. Remove the background fabric from the light box and anchor it with pins or tape over a piece of smooth muslin on a flat surface. Now that you have stabilized the fabric, fill in the letters or darken some parts of the letters to make them stand out (fig. 1). Black ink is strong and historically appropriate. Brown is softer and also accurate because it imitates the sepia color of faded black lettering.

EMBELLISHING APPLIQUÉS

I love to embellish the flowers and leaves of my designs with ink. It is fun and easy to do, and I recommend that you try it. An element as small as the rosebud in Summer Roses can benefit from a touch of the pen (fig. 2). I shaded the edges of the calyx and the curl of the rose petal.

Fig. 1. Fill in the traced letters.

Fig. 2. The calyx is shaded with green ink, the rosebud with red ink, and veins are added to the leaves.

Fig. 3. Inked details on Scottish Thistle (pattern on page 58)

Fig. 4. Stamped element from Bowl of Tulips (pattern on page 36)

I used the same technique to shade the tiny flowers and add veins to the tiny leaves in Scottish Thistle.

While I loved the mottled green fabric in Scottish Thistle, it seemed a bit dull after I finished sewing it. The solution . . . a touch of ink to highlight the shape of the leaves. I shaded the points of the flower, too (fig. 3).

Use fabric pens to add details and shading to your flowers and leaves. It is easier to do this before you cut out the element because the larger piece of uncut fabric can be stabilized with removable tape.

Follow these steps to add inked details to your appliqué elements:

1. Mark the sewing outline of the petals or leaves on your appliqué fabric. Do not cut the piece yet.

2. To stabilize the fabric, lay the fabric over a piece of smooth muslin.

3. Make light strokes with the side of the pen rather than the point.

4. Practice on scrap fabric to learn to control the strength of the color.

5. Let the ink dry then iron the inking with a dry iron to heat-set it.

6. Cut out the appliqué element and sew it in place.

ADDING STAMPED IMAGES

You may notice that, on each of the twelve blocks in the BALTIMORE'S COUNTRY COUSINS quilt, there is a tiny stamped image (fig. 4).

These embellishments are purely decorative, and I added them just for fun. Most of the stamps are craft/paper stamps, but several are Victorian-style images that I designed. Until a good fabric ink was developed, I would not stamp my quilts because the resolution and clarity were unreliable. However, just at the time I was finishing this quilt top, a wonderful fabric ink came on the market, and BALTIMORE'S COUNTRY COUSINS became my first stamped quilt.

Stamping on quilts can add a lovely, delicate touch. The stamping can also be useful, if you use it as a way to add signatures to a quilt. Stamped signatures surrounded by decorative cartouches were used on many of the signature quilts of the mid-nineteenth century.

The stamping must be done on the blocks or the quilt top before it is sandwiched with the batting and backing. To get good resolution and a well-defined image, stamp on a hard, flat surface. Practice on scrap fabric to learn how much ink to put on the stamp pad, how hard to press on the fabric, and how to lift the stamp without smearing any ink.

You will need the following supplies for your quilt project:

→ Stamp (it can be a detailed design)

→ Fabric ink pad

→ Stamp cleaner (hand wipes work well, too)

Follow these steps to stamp your block:

1. Have your supplies nearby, but not where anything can spill on the fabric.

2. Lay the fabric on a flat, smooth surface and anchor it with removable tape.

3. Ink the stamp by repeatedly tamping the stamp on the ink pad.

4. Press the stamp on the fabric without rocking or moving the stamp.

5. Lift the stamp carefully and directly upward.

6. Let the ink dry for a few hours.

7. Heat-set the ink with a dry iron or in a clothes dryer.

Fig. 4. Stamped element from Unbroken Circle (pattern on page 40)

COUNTRY COUSINS
Variations

Fig. 1. UNBROKEN CIRCLE MEDALLION. The circle makes a dramatic center for a simple medallion.

Fig. 2. BELOVED HEART MEDALLION. Hearts and a crisp dogtooth edge make lovely border elements.

All the blocks are so lovely that they can be used individually or in various combinations in many other projects. You can also take appliqué elements from the blocks and combine them.

MEDALLION WALLHANGINGS

Each block can stand alone as the center of a one-block wallhanging. Consider enlarging a block and adding a border. The simplest border would be a stripe or large print, chosen to coordinate with the block design and the fabrics.

One way to create a spectacular border is by including some elements from the block. Just as I repeated the flowers, leaves, and other block elements in the border of BALTIMORE'S COUNTRY COUSINS, you can do the same to create borders for small quilts.

The bull's-eye motif in the Unbroken Circle block (page 40) makes an ideal border element. Repeat the color and scale in the border, and you have a lovely small quilt design (fig. 1).

Beloved Heart is another lovely design that can stand alone. The hearts in the border corners are from Crossed Hearts (page 33), but you can cut any heart to fit your border (fig. 2).

The large flowers in Drooping Daisies (page 28) beg to be corner designs. Repeating them in the four corners of a border adds the finishing touch to the small quilt shown in figure 3.

Fruitful Pear Tree (page 48) is one of my favorite blocks, and it can happily stand alone as the center of a special quilt. Because it has such a graceful spread of hanging fruit, you can continue this theme in the border. Figure 4 shows that, often, decorating only two corners is more effective than filling all four sides or corners.

Home Sweet Home is the perfect block for a housewarming gift (fig. 5). I couldn't resist surrounding it with well-known phrases about home, all written in the border. See page 14 for instructions on tracing letters on fabric.

Consider combining elements from several blocks to create an extraordinary design, such as the tall flower vines placed on either side of the house in Home Sweet Home. This pair of vines would look lovely bracketing any block, but it is particularly fanciful with the Birds at the Fountain block (fig. 6, page 20).

HOME DECOR

The only block set on point, Striped Flower Basket, looks wonderful in a table runner. The runner can be any length, with the baskets placed at either end facing inward or outward. The width of the table runner is determined by the width of the blocks set on point. Consider bordering the two blocks or the entire runner. A striped or checked fabric would make a lovely border. Construction is easy, and the simplest assembly method is shown in figure 7, page 21.

You can also use three blocks to create a stunning, long wall quilt (fig. 8, page 21).

Fig. 3. DROOPING DAISIES MEDALLION. Echo the block elements in the border corners.

Fig. 4. FRUITFUL PEAR TREE MEDALLION. Drape pears and leaves in two corners only.

Fig. 5. HOME SWEET HOME. Writing in the borders can be an effective embellishment.

Fig. 6. You can make a rectangular quilt by adding borders to the sides. Here I used the vines from HOME SWEET HOME.

CLOTHING AND ACCESSORIES

The individual appliqué elements in the sixteen blocks provide a wealth of designs that would fit nicely into many other sewing projects (fig. 9). The patterns contain a variety of birds, flowers, leaves, and hearts, any of which can be combined or used as the inspiration for a lovely tote bag, item of clothing, or small sewing accessory. Consider, too, the different layouts of leaves and vines. Because of their lovely shapes, these can be adapted to enhance other projects.

Table runner by Jacqueline Biegel

Table runner by Talin N. Biesel

Fig. 7. Table runner assembly

Fig. 8. Three-block wall quilt assembly

Fig. 9. Appliqué elements from the blocks can be used in many projects, such as this tote bag designed by Lacey Hill.

TRIPLE BASKETS wall quilt by Maureen Papola

MAKING THE
Quilt

The BALTIMORE'S COUNTRY COUSINS quilt is pictured on page 4.

Quilt size: 70" x 87 ½"
Block size: 16" x 16"

I recommend including several prints of each color. If you are buying new fabric for this project, buy all the fabric for the quilt at one time to guarantee continuity among the blocks. Don't be afraid to buy too much fabric. (That's how you amass a usable fabric collection.) For any major quilt project, it's a good idea to buy plenty of each fabric so you are sure to have some left for those last blocks.

COLOR NOTES

 Block background: A subtle, printed fabric makes a lovely background, and a dark background creates a dramatic quilt. If you plan to write or stamp on the blocks, choose white, ecru, or a light color. You can use the same fabric for the outer border if you are planning to appliqué it.

 Greens and browns: For variety in the leaves and stems, I used five different green prints in medium and dark values, ranging in color from yellow greens to dark hunter greens. In some blocks, I used browns for the stems.

 Reds: For the flowers, hearts, and details, I used many different red prints but kept all of them rich and vivid.

 Yellows: I also used several yellow prints, from gold to clear yellow, in the flowers, hearts, and details.

 Blues: Choose at least two values for the birds so the wings stand out against their bodies. Choose several other blues for the vases and details.

 Pinks: Used infrequently, pink adds panache! I used reproductions of the bright double pinks (bubble gum pinks) of the 1800s.

 Sashing and inner border: I recommend waiting until all the blocks are finished to decide on the sashing. I used red, a warm color, which makes a strong grid on the quilt. Any color would be fine. Decide whether you want the sashing to make a strong statement, as the bright red does, or to act as a background to make the blocks stand out; in the latter case, choose a cool or soft color.

Outer border without appliqué: As with the sashing, I recommend waiting to decide on the border fabric to allow you to see the quilt as a whole. Then you can decide what the border can do to enhance the quilt blocks. If you have worked from a theme fabric (described on page 7), it makes a wonderful border choice because it will echo the colors in the quilt center.

Fabric Requirements

	FABRIC	YARDS	CUT
	Background* and	5½	12 squares 18" x 18"
	Appliquéd border*		2 strips 10" x 72½"
			2 strips 10" x 74"
	Greens and browns for stems and leaves	scraps	patterns
	Vine	⅝	1 square 20" x 20"
	Reds for flowers, hearts, and details	scraps	patterns
	Yellows for flowers, hearts, and details	scraps	patterns
	Blues for birds, vases, and details	scraps	patterns
	Pinks for flowers and hearts	scraps	patterns
	Sashing and	2⅛	3 strips 2" x 51½"
			8 strips 2" x 16½"
	Inner border		2 strips 2" x 56½"
			2 strips 2" x 71"
	Backing	5½	2 panels 39" x 94"
	Binding	¾	9 strips 2½" x 42"
	*If you prefer a plain fabric outer border, buy 3¼ yd. for block backgrounds and 2¼ yd. for the border. All outer border strips include 2" extra length for insurance.		

QUILT BODY ASSEMBLY

1. Select 12 block patterns for your quilt (patterns begin on page 25) and enlarge them 160% to make 16" finished blocks.

2. Use your favorite method to appliqué the blocks. The author's method is described beginning on page 10. Trim the blocks to 16½".

3. Referring to the Fabric Requirements table, cut the sashing pieces for your quilt.

4. Arrange the blocks and sashing pieces then sew them together in rows. Join the rows to complete the quilt body (see quilt assembly diagram, page 24).

BORDER ASSEMBLY

1. Read the Appliquéing the Border directions on page 12. Cut the pieces listed in the Border Appliqué Elements table on page 24.

2. Arrange and sew the vine on the strips, leaving a 5" tail free to sew later. Keep in mind that the finished borders will be 8" wide (fig. 7, page 13).

3. Appliqué the border elements to the border strips, but wait to add the corner elements and sew the ends of the vines until the borders have been sewn to the quilt.

Quilt assembly

4. Press the border strips and trim them to 8½" wide. (Trim equally from both long edges to keep the design centered.

5. Measure the quilt's length and cut the side border strips to that measurement. Sew these strips to the sides of the quilt.

6. Measure the quilt's width, including the side borders, and cut the remaining two border strips that length. Sew these to the top and bottom, then appliqué the corners.

FINISHING

Layer the quilt top, batting, and backing. Baste and quilt the layers. Use double-fold, continuous binding (or your preferred method) to bind the raw edges of the quilt.

Border Appliqué Elements			
ELEMENT	**FROM PATTERN**	**MAKE**	**COLORS**
Birds	Four Feeding Birds, p. 27	2 (1 reverse)	blue
Lg. red flowers	Drooping Daisies, p. 29	4	red petals, yellow centers
Bull's-eyes	Unbroken Circle, p. 41	12	red, yellow, blue circles
Pears	Fruitful Pear Tree, p. 49	12	yellows
Pear leaves	Fruitful Pear Tree, p. 49	12	greens
Daisy leaves	Drooping Daisies, p. 29	41	greens
Small flowers	Drooping Daisies, p. 29	12	8 blue, 4 red
Tiny hearts	Four Feeding Birds, p. 27	2	red
Tiny flowers	Striped Basket, p. 51	18	petals in various colors
Large hearts	Crossed Hearts, p. 33	4	red
Vine	(Finishes ⅛" x ¼" wide)	1" x 350"	green

BLOCK
Patterns

In addition to the twelve blocks in the BALTIMORE'S COUNTRY COUSINS quilt, I have designed four more lovely blocks in the same style, which can be used in combination with the original twelve for your projects. All of the patterns are sized for a 12" block, but you can resize them as desired (see the Block Sizing chart).

Here are some tips for using the patterns:

✦ I recommend that you use 11" x 17" paper to trace a complete block pattern.

✦ The center of each pattern is marked.

✦ Dashed lines mark the horizontal and vertical centers of each block.

✦ For symmetrical patterns, only half of the pattern is given. To make a pattern for the whole design, fold a vertical centerline in your paper. Unfold the paper and match the vertical centerline so it is easy to see. Refold the paper and put it over a light table or a window, so you can see your tracing through the folded paper. Retrace your tracing on the other half of the paper. This method guarantees that the two sides will be exactly the same.

✦ Be sure to mark the center, vertical, and horizontal lines, and any diagonal lines on your tracing.

✦ To trace a circular pattern, mark (but don't fold) a vertical centerline on your paper. Trace the pattern, including the placement lines, on the appropriate side of this centerline. Keep the pattern face up and turn it 180 degrees to trace the second side.

Block Sizing	
SIZE	ENLARGEMENT
14"	140%
16"	160%
18"	180%
20"	200%
22"	220%
24"	240%

Four Feeding Birds

COLOR CONSIDERATIONS

This block offers little room for variety in fabric or color, so choose interesting prints for the large elements (leaves and birds) to add texture and interest. Use the center elements and small leaves to echo the color of the four tiny hearts, which will add a bit of contrast and sparkle to the green and blue leaves and birds.

TRACING THE PATTERN

To complete the tracing of this circle, keep the pattern face up and turn it four times to complete the design. Line up the center-lines and trace.

STITCHING SEQUENCE

This is an easy block to sew because the shapes are simple and there are few of them. To line up the birds' beaks, the hearts, and the stems, appliqué them in this order:

1. Center circle: You can sew the flower on the center circle either before or after *appliquéing the circle to the background.*

2. Four small center leaves

3. Stems: Cut the stems a bit too long. Sew both sides along the center of the stem but leave both ends dangling so you can adjust and trim them later.

4. Large leaves: Tuck the stem ends under the leaves then sew the leaves in place.

5. Birds' bodies

6. Hearts: Be sure to adjust their positions so they touch the birds' beaks. Tuck the stem ends under the hearts and trim the stems. Adjust the stem curves as necessary.

7. Embroider or ink the birds' eyes (optional).

Drooping Daisies

STITCHING SEQUENCE

1. Stems: Leave long tails.

2. Basket: Mark and cut a full piece of the red. Mark and cut the yellow crown. Appliqué the yellow over the red, leaving the edges free to be sewn to the background later. Sew the blue bottom strip over the base of the basket. Appliqué the entire basket unit to the background, trimming and covering the stem ends.

3. Flower petals: These need to touch the stem ends.

4. Yellow dots: Cover the petal and stem ends.

5. Leaves

6. Bird: Once the flowers and leaves are sewn in place, center the bird between them, adjusting its position, and even its size, as necessary.

COLOR CONSIDERATIONS

The large flowers and the basket are the main elements, so place the strongest colors there. Consider making the drooping lower flowers or their dots out of the same color as the bird to prevent isolating the bird. Try to repeat every color somewhere else in the block. This will carry the viewer's eye around the block.

in these elements in the tiny hearts, in the circle at the bottom, and perhaps in some of the leaves. The bottom circle could even be replaced by the flower pattern, thus picking up two of the colors and making the bottom of the block stronger. Just move or eliminate some of the leaves to allow for the larger flower and be sure to plan the writing around it.

STITCHING SEQUENCE

1. **Stems**

2. **Flowers**

3. **Circle** (or flower) at the base

4. **Leaves and hearts**

5. **Bird:** Hand piece or appliqué the bird's tummy to his body before sewing the bird to the background. When you sew the body to the background, leave an opening for inserting the bottom wing. Add the wings last.

Garden Medallion

WRITING IN THE CENTER

This block contains an open center in which to write documentation. It makes the perfect center block in a Nine-Patch quilt, but as you can see in my version of BALTIMORE'S COUNTRY COUSINS, a block with writing doesn't have to be in the center of the quilt. It looks lovely in any position. Your writing doesn't have to be beautiful either. It's what is said that counts. Use a black permanent pen with a moderately large point (.05 or larger) for this large space.

COLOR CONSIDERATIONS

There are only three large elements in this block: the bird and the two flowers on either side of it. Try to repeat the colors used

Garden Medallion

POSSIBLE ADDITIONS

If you find the block too simple, add pairs of small hearts from Four Feeding Birds (page 26) at the bases of the large hearts or add more small leaves at the bases of the hearts.

Crossed Hearts

STITCHING SEQUENCE

1. **Stems**

2. **Center flower:** Cover stems.

3. **Circle flower center**

4. **Hearts:** Cover stems.

5. **Leaves and small hearts,** if desired.

COLOR CONSIDERATIONS

This simple block offers little opportunity to play with color. Therefore, choose interesting, large prints for the hearts and the center flower. Vary the leaf fabrics in prints and shades of green.

Beloved Heart

1. **Center heart:** Mark all sewing/turn lines on the yellow and red heart fabrics. Appliqué the outside edge of the red heart over the gold one. For the reverse appliqué (marked RA on the pattern), carefully slit the red fabric between the lines and appliqué the edges to reveal the gold base.

2. **Corner green leaves**

3. **Corner red wings**

4. **Corner yellow dots:** Cover wings and leaves.

5. **Hearts on leaf tips:** These are very tiny, and the leaves look perfectly fine without them, if you prefer. Or, you can use buttons, stuffed berries, or circles.

COLOR CONSIDERATIONS

This three-color block is quite straightforward, with red and green brightened by yellow accents.

RA

RA

1. **Center stem**

2. **Side stems**

3. **Tulips:** The tulips can be appliquéd or hand pieced as units, then appliquéd to the background. For hand piecing, mark the sewing lines on the backs of the fabrics instead of the front. Be sure to stop sewing at the cross seams, leaving the seam allowances unsewn.

4. **Top center flower**

5. **Bowl**

6. **Leaves:** Adjust their angles or sizes slightly to fit the space.

7. **Hearts on the bowl:** These can be appliquéd or reverse appliquéd. For accurate spacing, sew the center heart first then the two outer ones. The last two can be evenly spaced between them. If you prefer, you can eliminate the hearts or have only three. The bowl will still look lovely!

8. Dots on the bowl, hearts on center stem, and center of center flower.

Bowl of Tulips

COLOR CONSIDERATIONS

Red and yellow flowers, green leaves, and a blue bowl create a balanced color design. If you want to add more blue or yellow, change the center round flower. Yellow hearts on the blue bowl would stand out more than the red ones.

2. **Vase:** Cover stem.

3. **Large leaves:** These can be simplified by rounding off the deep indentations and using gentle curves for their shapes.

4. **Large flowers:** Two sides and one center.

5. **Small leaves:** Adjust their angles to leave space between the elements.

6. **Vines:** Use three strands of dark green floss to embroider the vines for the berries, shortening them, if necessary.

7. **Berries and small leaves:** Consider adding more berries.

Leaves & Berries

COLOR CONSIDERATIONS

This block has only two colors, red and green. To create interest in this simple color scheme, use interesting prints in the large pieces: the vase, large leaves, and flowers, or use different colors in the center flower and berries to totally change the look.

STITCHING SEQUENCE

1. **Stems:** Lay out, pin or baste, and sew the center stem and side stems in position, with the center stem covering the ends of the side stems.

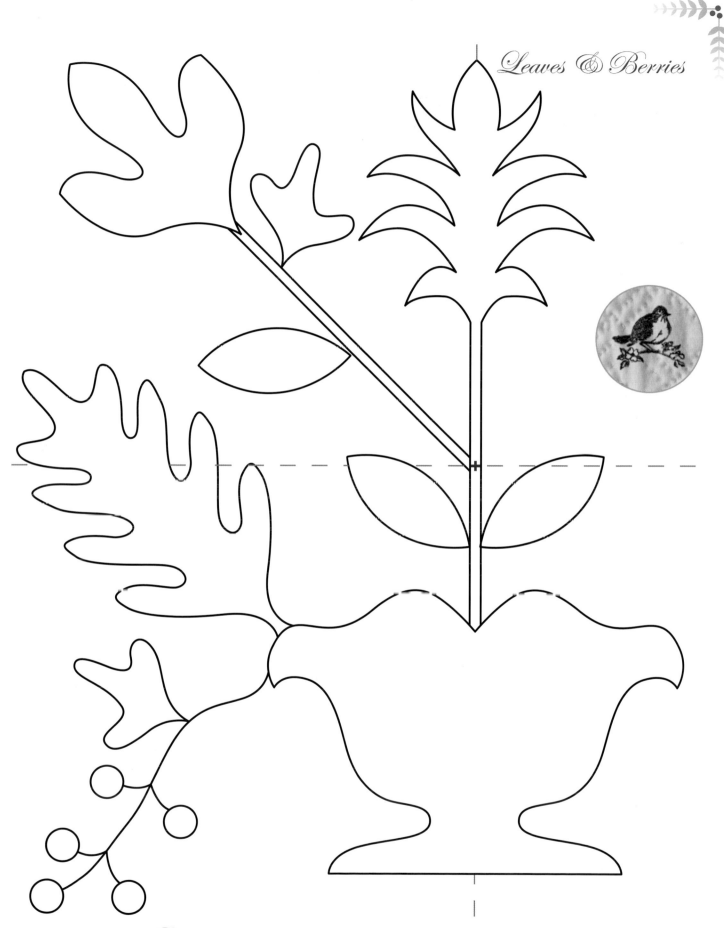

1. **Center bull's-eye:** Consider sewing the circles together as a unit before appliquéing the bull's-eye to the background.

2. **Wreath stem**

3. **Corner bull's-eyes:** These, too, can be sewn as units before applying them to the background.

4. **Hearts:** Adjust their positions, if necessary, so they are evenly spaced and aligned on the diagonal.

5. **Large corner leaves:** Align with the diagonal guides.

6. **Leaves around the wreath:** Do not tuck these under the stem. The points are part of the beauty of the block. Adjust the spacing, if necessary.

Unbroken Circle

COLOR CONSIDERATIONS

Include in this block most or all of the fabrics you have used in other blocks. To give the block a bright, folksy feel, use a great variety of green leaf fabrics and add a few yellow and blue leaves. Scatter the differently colored leaves randomly around the circle. For the bull's-eyes, use bright, high-contrast colors, a gradation of one color, or a set of analogous colors (adjacent on the color wheel).

TRACING THE PATTERN

To complete the tracing of this circle, keep the pattern face up and rotate it as needed to trace the four sections. Line up the center lines and trace.

Birds at the Fountain

3. Birds: Appliqué the bodies, then position and sew the wings on top.

4. Urns: Cut the handle openings when marking the vase outline. Appliqué them to the background immediately after cutting because the handles are fragile. The handles can be eliminated or widened if they are too narrow to sew comfortably.

5. Bubbles: Adjust their spacing as necessary between the birds and the waterspout.

6. Flowers, leaves, and cherries

7. Use three strands of floss to embroider the stems and the birds' legs, if desired. Sew these last so you can adjust them to fill between the flowers and berries.

8. Ground (optional): Adjust its height to fit the block. Leave extra fabric so it can be trimmed when you put the blocks together. If you prefer, the fountain can float in the block without the strip of ground, just as the containers do in other blocks.

COLOR CONSIDERATIONS

This block can accommodate a great variety of fabrics, so pick up fabrics from the other blocks to use here. Use the strongest colors for the birds and the fountain, so they stand out. The rest of the design is subordinate to these elements.

STITCHING SEQUENCE

1. **Water spout**

2. **Fountain base:** Add decorative stars *before appliquéing the base to the background.*

Home Sweet Home

COLOR CONSIDERATIONS

A red house will stand out. Use blue for the bird body and echo the red house with another red or a pink in the bird's wing and the flowers. Use brown or green for the vine and a variety of greens for the leaves. Use brown or black for the chimney caps (could be ribbon). For the lawn, alternate a green print and a flower print. This lawn can be eliminated, or a curved path can be substituted.

STITCHING SEQUENCE

1. **House:** Appliqué the roof and door onto the house. Cut away the house fabric behind the roof and door. Mark and clip inside the four corners of each window to reverse appliqué later. Sew the house to the background, inserting the two chimney bases as you sew along the top roof edge.

2. **Windows:** Use ⅛" black grosgrain ribbon for the window sashes. Pin the ribbon strips under the house fabric to hold them in place then catch them in the appliqué stitches as you sew the windows. Reverse appliqué the window and door openings, catching the ribbon ends.

3. **Chimney caps**

4. **Stems**

5. **Flowers and their centers**

6. **Lawn:** Piece a 16" long strip, alternating pieces of 1" wide green fabric and 2" wide floral fabric. Position the strip so a floral piece is in the center, under the door. Sew the strip along the bottom of the block, covering the bases of the house and the stems.

7. **Bird:** Appliqué the body, centering it between the flowers. Sew the wing on top.

8. **Leaves and berries**

9. **Smoke (optional):** The smoke can be appliquéd or inked in with a black permanent-ink pen (.01).

10. French knots would make good berries in the bird's mouth.

Home Sweet Home

Home Sweet Home

Fruitful Pear Tree

1. Tree: The tree is symmetrical. Because the limbs are narrow, use a freezer-paper template ironed on the right side of the fabric. Mark the freezer paper on the dull side, cut it on the line, iron it on the tree fabric, and mark the fabric, staying close to the freezer paper. On dark brown, use a yellow or blue pencil to make a clear, easily hidden turn line.

If the limbs seem too narrow for you to appliqué, make them a little wider when you mark them. The tree will still look wonderful. With the freezer paper still attached to the fabric, cut the tree, leaving a ⅛"–³⁄₁₆" turn-under allowance. Peel off the freezer paper and appliqué the tree to the background.

2. Pears and leaves: Because all of the pears and leaves are the same shape and size, scatter the different fabrics around the block to create balance and movement.

COLOR CONSIDERATIONS

Because this is such a simple block with only three colors, you can create variety by using interesting shaded prints. For the pears, use several gold fabrics. To create blushing, rounded pears, include fabrics that contain a *gradated* pattern or use yellow-pink hand-dyed fabrics or batiks. For the leaves, use a variety of greens.

TRACING THE PATTERN

This block is almost symmetrical, except for the positions of one pear and one leaf at the center top and the shape of the trunk base. These pieces are shaded on the pattern.

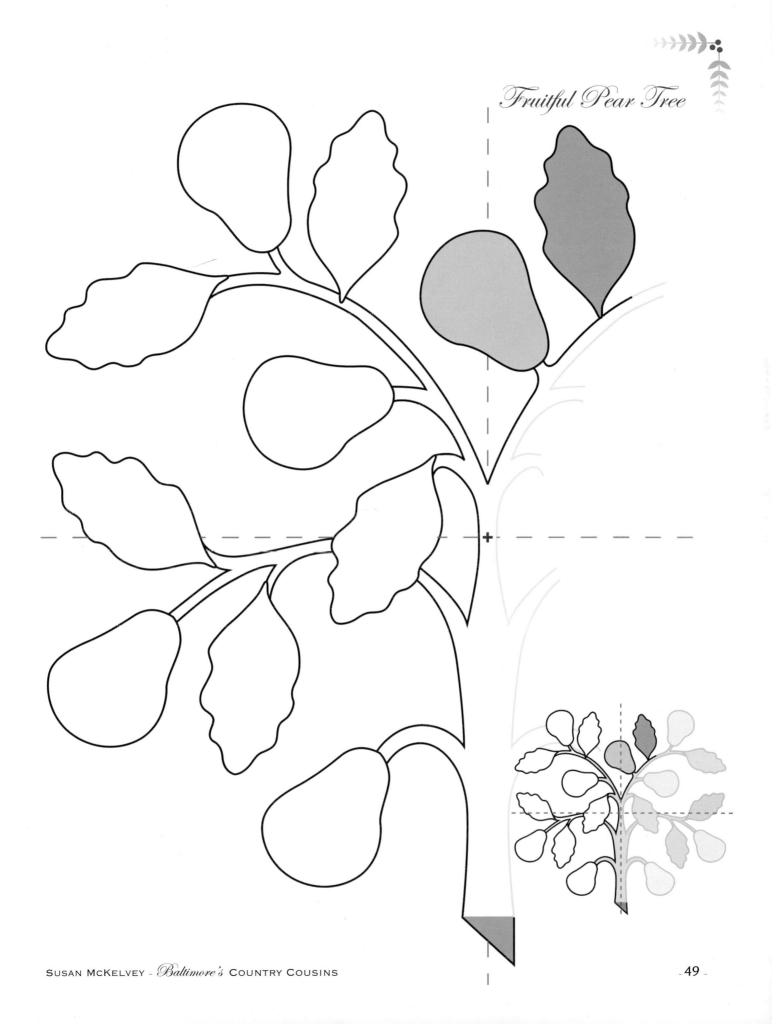

other blocks. Tuck in some pink, baby blue, and yellow leaves between the green ones. For the petals of the little flowers, use three colors or at least three fabrics.

STITCHING SEQUENCE

1. **Center stem**

2. **Side stems**

3. **Center flower:** Cover the stems.

4. **Basket:** Machine or hand-piece the strips (it's fast and easy). Add the handles and base then appliqué the basket as a unit to the background.

5. **Small flowers**

6. **Leaves**

Striped Flower Basket

BLOCK SETTING

This is the only block in the quilt set on the diagonal. I adore it because it's so cheerful, and it comes right out of the 1850s. Quiltmakers often threw in an odd block, and this one is mine. Consider using it in the four corners of a nine- or sixteen-block quilt (see page 18 for more ideas).

COLOR CONSIDERATIONS

There are five fabrics in the basket, three different colors for the center area, plus bright red handles and a navy blue scalloped base. Go wild with variety on the leaves. Repeat fabrics from

MORE
Patterns

Sunflowers & Sweet Peas

COLOR CONSIDERATIONS

Sunflowers have brown centers and bright yellow-gold petals. For the three petals of the sweet peas, use gradations of pale and bright pinks and lavenders or use your own color combination. In the vase, pick up a bit of yellow and any colors you want to emphasize from other blocks. The stems and leaves look nice in a variety of greens.

STITCHING SEQUENCE

1. Stems and four large center leaves: Pin or baste the four leaves in place, leaving the ends loose and long enough to tuck under the center stem. (Leave a ¼" opening at the outer top edge of the top leaves for the side stems.) Pin or baste the drooping side stems, leaving the ends loose to tuck under the center stem. Sew these leaves and stems.

2. Center sunflower: Cover the stem.

3. Drooping sunflowers: Cover the stems.

4. Vase: Appliqué the three parts of the vase together to make a unit. Then sew the unit to the background, covering the stems.

5. Sweet peas: Overlap the petals and cover the stems.

6. Small sweet pea leaves

STITCHING SEQUENCE

1. All stems: Tuck the side stem ends under the center stem.

2. Basket: Use reverse appliqué to combine two fabrics for the basket, or use a single fabric with gradations of color instead. Sew the basket to the background, covering the stem.

3. Appliqué the two parts of each flower together to make units. Then sew the units to the background.

4. Center flower

5. Outer flowers

6. Leaves: Note there are three sizes of leaves. Make sure the top two leaves cover the top of the center stem. Adjust the leaf spacing to fit among the flowers.

Basket of Bluebells

COLOR CONSIDERATIONS

This is a simple coloration. Make the bluebells in shades of blue and white, the basket in any color combination, and the leaves and stems in various greens. Use a variety of fabrics and values to create a pretty block.

Basket of Bluebells

RA RA

2. Roses: Appliqué the layers from the bottom up to make single units. Don't sew the two side roses on their stems until you have sewn all the leaves. You may need to adjust their positions. Appliqué the center unit to the background.

3. Basket: Piece or appliqué the vertical strips. Then sew that part of the basket to the background. Add the top and bottom strips, covering the stems as well as the raw edges of the basket

4. Rosebuds and leaves

Summer Roses

COLOR CONSIDERATIONS

Use shades of red, rose, pink, or yellow for the roses and buds and a variety of greens and browns for the leaves and stems.

STITCHING SEQUENCE

1. Stems: Embroider the top pair of stems if you want them to be delicate. Appliqué the rest.

Summer Roses

1. Center stem with attached leaves: Leave the top open to insert the flower. Also leave places to insert the side stems.

2. Side stems

3. Small flowers and tiny leaves

4. Vase: Appliqué the three parts of the vase to make a unit. Appliqué the unit to the background, covering the stem. Be sure to leave space below the small flowers.

Scottish Thistle

COLOR CONSIDERATIONS

Use green for the leaves and red, rose, or pink for the thistle. Choose any colors for the small flowers. Use strong colors in the vase, either shadings of a color or highly contrasting colors.

Scottish Thistle

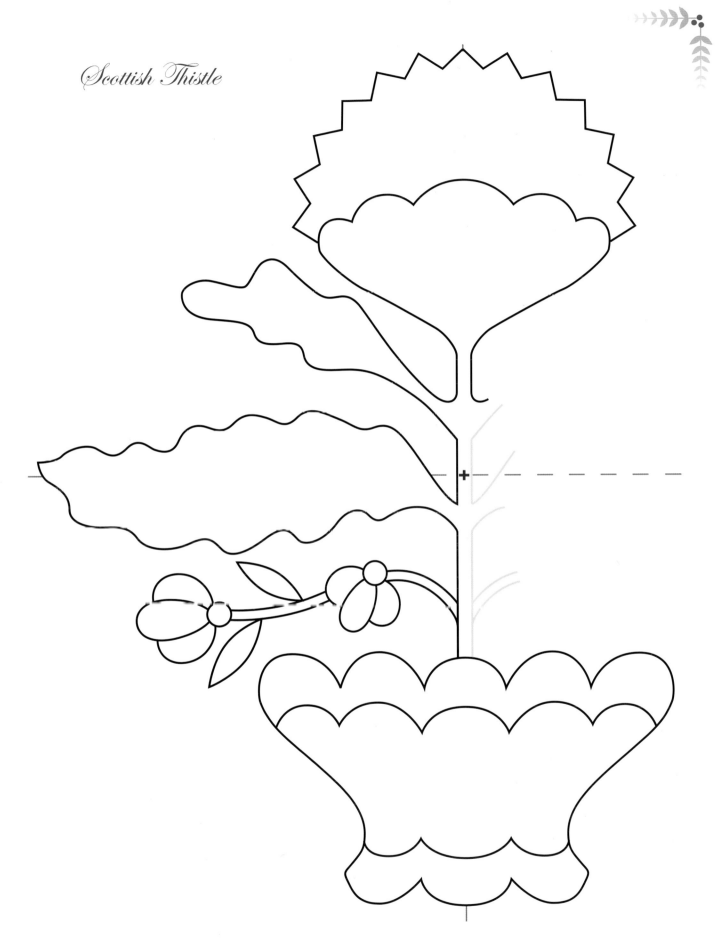

THE Quiltmakers

I would like to thank the women who made samples for this book. Their generosity with time and talent greatly contributed to the beauty of the quilts and blocks included here. Although there was not space for all of the lovely items they made, I hope the making may serve as partial reward. My sincere gratitude to all of you.

Jacqueline Biegel of Paramus, New Jersey, a member of the Brownstone Quilters

Talin Biesel of Wyckoff, New Jersey, a member of the Brownstone Quilters

Jan Carlson of Severna Park, Maryland, a founding member of the Baltimore Appliqué Society

Lacey Hill of Hillsdale, New Jersey, a member of the Brownstone Quilters

Maureen Papola of Ridgewood, New Jersey, a member of the Brownstone Quilters

Candy Stiffler of Trappe, Maryland, a member of The Bayside Quilters

BALTIMORE ON THE LESS TRAVELED BACK ROADS, 50" x 50", by Jan Carlson

IN BLOOMING COLORS, 52" x 52", by Candy Stiffler

Bibliography

Cory, Pepper, and Susan McKelvey. *The Signature Quilt.* Saddle Brook, NJ: Quilt House Publishing, 1995.

Duke, Dennis, and Deborah Harding. *America's Glorious Quilts.* New York: Park Lane, 1987.

Katzenberg, Dena. *Baltimore Quilts.* Baltimore: The Baltimore Museum of Art, 1981.

Kiracoffe, Roderick. *The American Quilt: A History of Cloth and Comfort 1750–1950.* New York: Clarkson Potter, 1993.

Lipman, Jean, and Alice Winchester. *The Flowering of American Folk Art: 1776–1876.* Philadelphia: Running Press Book Publishers, 1974.

Seaman-Allen, Gloria, and Nancy Gibson-Tuckhorn. *A Maryland Album.* Nashville: Rutledge Hill Press, 1995.

Warren, Elizabeth T., and Sharon L. Eusenstat. *Glorious American Quilts.* New York: Penguin Studio, 1996.

Zegart, Terri. *Quilts: An American Heritage.* New York: Smithmark, 1994.

— *Quilts and Quiltmakers Covering Connecticut.* Atglen, PA: Schiffer Ltd., 2002.

McKelvey, Susan. *A Treasury of Quilt Labels.* Lafayette, CA: C&T Publishing, 1993.

—. *Color for Quilters II.* Millersville, MD: Wallflower Designs, 1993.

—. *EQ Color.* Bowling Green, OH: The Electric Quilt Company, 2003.

—. *Fancy Feathered Friends for Quilters.* Paducah, KY: American Quilter's Society, 2003.

—. *Friendship's Offering.* Lafayette, CA: C&T Publishing, 1987.

Resources

JUKEBOX
P.O. Box 1518
Tustin, CA 92781-1518
jukeboxquilts.com

Fabric pens and painting supplies

**WALLFLOWER DESIGNS BY
SUSAN MCKELVEY**
smckelvey@toad.net

Books and supplies for writing and drawing on fabric

Sunflowers & Sweet Peas, by Candy Stiffler

ABOUT THE
Author

Susan McKelvey has been quilting since 1976, when she made her first quilt, a Dresden Plate. When she moved to the Washington, D.C., area in 1977, she joined a thriving quilting community, active in the quilt revival. She became a founding member of the New Image Quilters, a group of professional quilters whose works were among the first accepted in art galleries in the Washington area.

Quilting and designing steadily since then, she has produced numerous pieces that have appeared in museums, galleries, and quilt shows throughout the United States. In 1987, she started her own company, Wallflower Designs.

In the days before quilting claimed her, Susan earned her B.A in English and Drama at Cornell College, and her M.A. in American Literature at the University of Chicago. She taught English at the secondary level for many years, including a two-year tour in Ethiopia as a Peace Corps volunteer.

Today, with their two children grown, Susan and her husband live on Maryland's rural eastern shore, where they and their pets enjoy all that the Chesapeake Bay has to offer. Susan's other interests include painting, writing, gardening, and volunteering with Golden Retriever Rescue.

Susan lectures and teaches about color, appliqué, and signature quilts throughout the United States at conferences and quilt guilds. She is the author of several books on these subjects. She is also the author of *Fancy Feathered Friends for Quilters,* published by AQS in 2003.

OTHER AQS *Books*

This is only a small selection of the books available from the American Quilter's Society. AQS books are known worldwide for timely topics, clear writing, beautiful color photos, and accurate illustrations and patterns. The following books are available from your local bookseller, quilt shop, or public library.

#6905   us$24.95

#6904   us$21.95

#6906   us$24.95

#6897   us$22.95

#6511   us$22.95

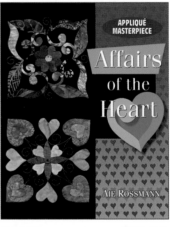

#6517   us$21.95

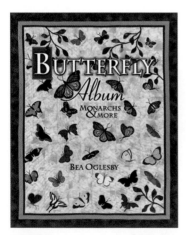

#6674   us$19.95

#6896   us$22.95

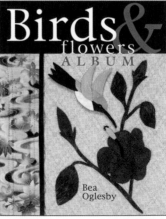

#6211   us$19.95

Look for these books nationally.
Call or **Visit** our Web site at

1-800-626-5420
www.AmericanQuilter.com